FABIANA ATTANASIO

MYTHOGRAPHIC

COLOR AND DISCOVER

Menagerie

AN ARTIST'S COLORING BOOK OF AMAZING ANIMALS

CASTLE POINT BOOKS
NEW YORK

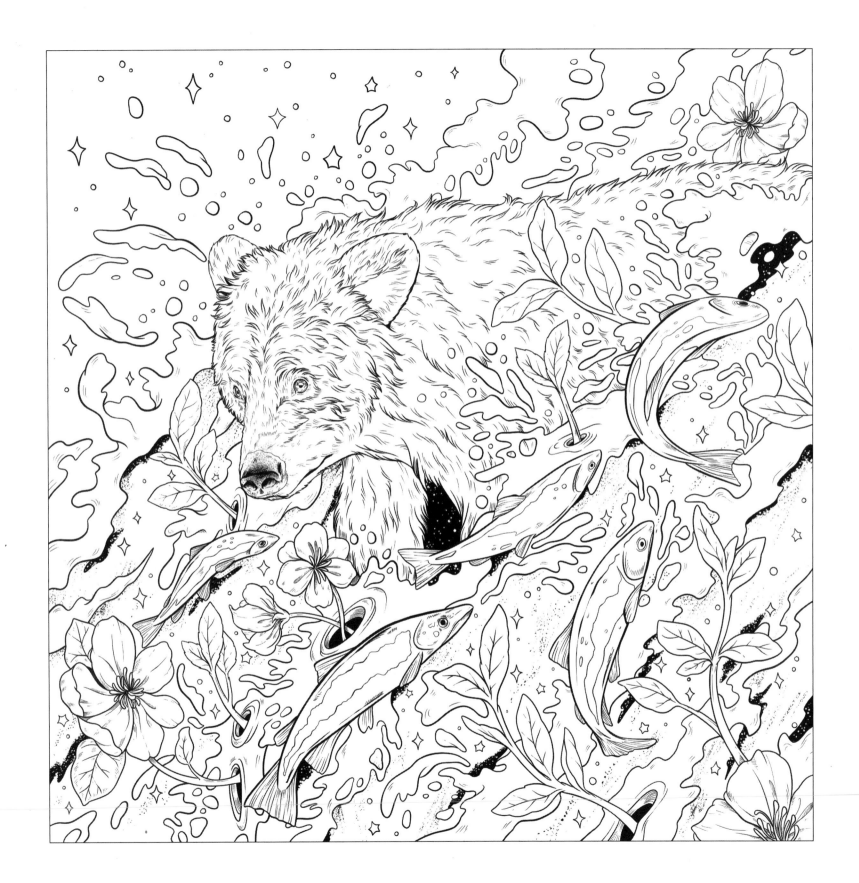

Discover more of Mythographic

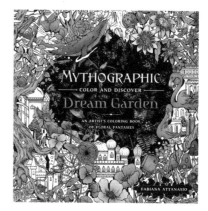

MYTHOGRAPHIC COLOR AND DISCOVER: MENAGERIE.
Copyright © 2022 by St. Martin's Press.
All rights reserved. Printed in Canada. For information, address
St. Martin's Publishing Group, 120 Broadway, New York, NY 10271.

www.castlepointbooks.com

The Castle Point Books trademark is owned by Castle Point Publishing, LLC.
Castle Point books are published and distributed by St. Martin's Publishing Group.

ISBN 978-1-250-28180-7 (trade paperback)

Cover design by Young Lim
Edited by Monica Sweeney

Our books may be purchased in bulk for promotional, educational, or business use.
Please contact your local bookseller or the Macmillan Corporate
and Premium Sales Department at 1-800-221-7945, extension 5442,
or by email at MacmillanSpecialMarkets@macmillan.com.

First Edition: 2022

10 9 8 7 6 5 4 3 2 1